T0132465

# How do YOU See God?

## Seeing God in ALL things

Suzette Montoya Sornborger

WestBow Press books may be ordered through booksellers or by contacting:

WestBow Press
A Division of Thomas Nelson & Zondervan
1663 Liberty Drive
Bloomington, IN 47403
www.westbowpress.com
844-714-3454

ISBN: 979-8-3850-0180-4 (sc)
ISBN: 979-8-3850-0181-1 (hc)
ISBN: 979-8-3850-0182-8 (e)

Library of Congress Control Number: 2023912121

Print information available on the last page.

WestBow Press rev. date: 8/28/2023

WESTBOW
PRESS®
A DIVISION OF THOMAS NELSON
& ZONDERVAN

To my familia...you have been an inspiration in my journey to capture the glory of God in everyday life. Thank you for supporting me along the way. Your trust, unwavering love, and reminders to be present in the moments of each day, with each of you, has made this a reality to hold and to share. God is amazing everyday, in all things and all ways!

I love you!

1

**Sammy** is a shy, curious boy who can't keep his head out of a book. His goofy, talkative, clever younger brother, Will, challenges him to look around and see the world. Josie, the middle sibling, is often distracted by whatever is in front of her. Mom, she is Mom. Sammy, Will, and Josie are waking up from a night's sleep. Mom comes in and hurries them along to get ready for school.

Mom says, "Kids, it's time to get up. We have to get ready for school."

Sammy replies, "OK, we're coming."

Sammy heads to the kitchen for breakfast with his head in a book. Will follows, trying to smack the book out of Sammy's hand. Josie skips behind, playing with her hair. They eat, brush their teeth, grab their lunches and backpacks, and head to the door.

Will says, "Mom, I forgot my glasses!" He runs to his room to get his glasses.

Mom asks, "Glasses? What glasses?"

Will replies, "My God glasses!" He makes two
circles with his fingers and puts them over
his eyes. "See, these are my God glasses. They
help me see and search for God in everything."
Pointing at things, he says, "See, look at
that cool bug on the step. Whoa, look at that
amazing orange butterfly. Mom, you should
try it."

Mom puts on her finger God glasses and plays along with Will.

Will asks, "So, Mom, what do you see with your God glasses?

Mom says, "Wow, Will, I guess that I haven't noticed the beautiful blooming tree across the street. Oh, and look at how dirty my car is!"

Josie says, "Mom, that's not a God thing; that's a car! You're funny, Mom."

Will pushes Sammy's book away from his face and says, "Sammy, put on your God glasses and tell us what you see."

Sammy is annoyed with Will but gives in and hands him his book to play along. "What am I supposed to be looking for again?'

Will says, "God things!"

Sammy says, "You mean like the trees and the squirrels? Stuff like that?"

Will says, "Yes! God things. God made all that!"

Sammy says, "OK, I see God things. Thanks, Will." Sammy takes his book back from Will and continues reading.

Will says, "Sammy, seriously, like what God things do you see?"

Sammy says, "I see the sky."

Will shakes his head, annoyed.

Josie yells, "What about me? Don't I get to put on *my* God glasses?"

Will says, "Sure, Josie, go ahead. What do you see?"

Josie replies, "I see birdies and bugs, and look, there's a dog! I see Mom pulling on my arm to get me in the car. OK, Mom, I'm coming."

Mom asks, "Everyone buckled in?"

Josie says, "Almost ... OK, now I am."

Mom asks, "Boys, are you good to go?"

The boys say, "Yes!"

Mom says, "OK, great. Will, thanks for reminding us of the importance of finding God in our rush this morning. That was a great start to the day! Where did you learn about your God glasses?"

Will replies, "Mrs. Madril talked about it in Sunday School. She asked each of us to share where we saw God in our day. Some kids seemed to have a hard time getting it, so she told us to put on God glasses. She said this would help us to see in a new way."

Mom says, "I like that Mrs. Madril. What a great idea!"

Josie says, "Hey, guys, look at that beautiful flag or kite thing."

Mom says, "That is beautiful, Josie. Thanks for pointing it out."

Will says, "Hey, Sammy, do you see God in the story of your book?"

Sammy looks up, annoyed yet curious about the question, and says, "Yes, actually, I do see God in my book. He's doing some cool things to help people."

Will says, "Awesome. God is pretty cool that way."

Josie says, "God *is* pretty cool. He helped my friend yesterday when she was sad."

Will asks, "How did He do that?"

Josie replies, "God gave her friends to hold her hand and be with her."

Mom says, "That's sweet, Josie. God is amazing. He reminds us that we are never alone!"

The car door opens, and Mom says, "Have a great day, guys. God bless you. Don't forget to put on your God glasses throughout the day. I want to hear all about where you saw God in your day today. I love you!"

Will says, "Bye, Mom, love you too."

Josie says, "Love you, Mom."

Sammy says, "Bye, Mom, thanks. Love you."

Printed in the United States
by Baker & Taylor Publisher Services